Learning to read. Reading to learn!

LEVEL ONE Sounding It Out Preschool–Kindergarten
For kids who know their alphabet and are starting to sound out words.

learning sight words • beginning reading • sounding out words

LEVEL TWO Reading with Help Preschool–Grade 1
For kids who know sight words and are learning to sound out new words.

expanding vocabulary • building confidence • sounding out bigger words

LEVEL THREE Independent Reading Grades 1–3
For kids who are beginning to read on their own.

introducing paragraphs • challenging vocabulary • reading for comprehension

LEVEL FOUR Chapters Grades 2–4
For confident readers who enjoy a mixture of images and story.

reading for learning • more complex content • feeding curiosity

Ripley Readers Designed to help kids build their reading skills and confidence at any level, this program offers a variety of fun, entertaining, and unbelievable topics to interest even the most reluctant readers. With stories and information that will spark their curiosity, each book will motivate them to start and keep reading.

Vice President, Licensing & Publishing Amanda Joiner
Editorial Manager Carrie Bolin

Editor Jordie R. Orlando
Designer Luis Fuentes
Reprographics Bob Prohaska

Chief Executive Officer Andy Edwards
Chief Commercial Officer Brett Clarke
Vice President, Global Licensing &
  Consumer Products Cassie Dombrowski
Vice President, Creative Dov Ribnik
Director, Brand & Athlete Marketing Ricky Melnik
Account Manager, Global Licensing &
  Consumer Products Andrew Hogan
Athlete Manager Chris Haffey
Special Thanks Ryan Williams

Published by Ripley Publishing 2020

10 9 8 7 6 5 4 3 2 1

ISBN: 978-1-60991-380-9

For more information regarding permission, contact:
VP Licensing & Publishing
Ripley Entertainment Inc.
7576 Kingspointe Parkway, Suite 188
Orlando, Florida 32819
Email: publishing@ripleys.com
www.ripleys.com/books

Manufactured in China in March 2020.

First Printing

Library of Congress Control Number: 2020931353

PUBLISHER'S NOTE
While every effort has been made to verify the accuracy of the entries in this book, the Publisher cannot be held responsible for any errors contained in the work. They would be glad to receive any information from readers.

WARNING
Some of the stunts and activities are undertaken by experts and should not be attempted by anyone without adequate training and supervision.

PHOTO CREDITS

Cover (bkg) © Vasyl Shulga/Shutterstock.com; (l, c) Photography by Mark Watson **3** Photography by Mark Watson **4** Photography by Mark Watson **5** Photography by Mark Watson **12-13** Photography by Mark Watson **14** Photography by Mark Watson **15** Photography by Josh Lynch **16** Photography by Sam Neill **17** Photography by Sam Neill **19** Photography by Andy Jackman **22** Photography by Mark Watson **25** Photography by Mark Watson **26-27** Photography by Nick Hamilton **30-31** Photography by Mark Watson

Key: t = top, b = bottom, c = center, l = left, r = right, bkg = background

All other photos are courtesy of Nitro Circus and Ryan Williams. Every attempt has been made to acknowledge correctly and contact copyright holders, and we apologize in advance for any unintentional errors or omissions, which will be corrected in future editions.

NITRO CIRCUS

NEVER DEFEATED!

FEATURING:
RYAN WILLIAMS

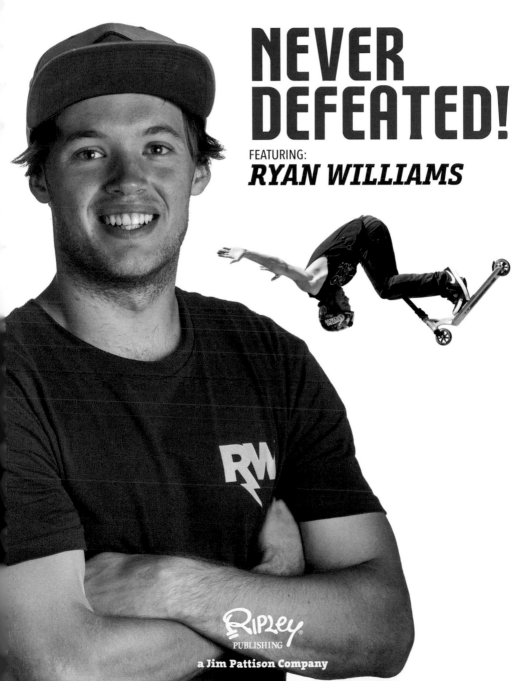

RIPLEY
PUBLISHING

a Jim Pattison Company

Ryan Williams loves to ride scooters and bikes with Nitro Circus!

His friends and fans call him R-Willy.

Ryan grew up on the Sunshine Coast of Australia. He liked to Rollerblade in skate parks when he was a kid.

Ryan started riding a scooter
when he was 12 years old.
He would practice for hours.

A lot of people thought scooters were just toys and not a real sport. They changed their minds after seeing Ryan ride and do amazing tricks!

Ryan rode his scooter at a skate park next to a bike track. He wanted to try that, too!

At 15 years old, he started riding a BMX bike.

All of that practice paid off! After a few years, he was so good that Nitro Circus invited him to show off his skills.

They were impressed and now R-Willy is part of the Nitro Circus family!

Ryan gets to tour the world with Nitro Circus. He has gone to places like France, New Zealand, Japan, and South Africa.

Seeing someone do flips off of a giant ramp is cool no matter where you are from!

When he is not doing shows with Nitro Circus, Ryan competes against other action sport athletes to see who can do the best tricks and jumps.

Ryan won Scooter Best Trick and BMX Best Trick at the 2017 Nitro World Games.

The next year, he won a gold medal at the X Games for jumping his bike higher than everyone else.

Way to go, R-Willy!

Ryan has done more world's first tricks than anyone! A world's first trick is a trick that no one else has ever done before.

BMX triple frontflip

Ryan is the first person to do a triple backflip on a scooter and a triple frontflip on a BMX bike.

Ryan has also created brand-new tricks. One of the coolest is the Free Willy, where he does a backflip while the scooter does a frontflip! They meet in the middle just in time to land safely.

Doing amazing tricks and winning medals seems to come easy for Ryan. But he will tell you that it takes hours and hours of practice.

It took him two years and over 100 tries before he landed the first Free Willy!

Sometimes it can be hard to keep practicing and Ryan can feel like a trick might be impossible. When he feels this way, he thinks of the people who look up to him.

He says, "Inspiring and helping the up-and-coming riders of today is what pushes me most to keep doing my best!"

Ryan is probably practicing for his next big trick right now! No matter how many times he fails, he will keep trying as long as it is safe.

Never defeated!

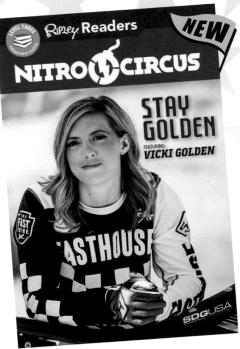